I Want to Talk With
my TEEN About

MOVIES,
MUSIC & MORE

BY
DR. WALT MUELLER

Standard®
PUBLISHING
Bringing The Word to Life

Cincinnati, Ohio

Credits

Credits
Produced by Susan Lingo Books™
Cover by Diana Walters
All Scripture quotations, unless otherwise
indicated, are taken from the HOLY BIBLE,
NEW INTERNATIONAL VERSION®.
NIV®. Copyright © 1973, 1978, 1984 by
International Bible Society. Used by permis-
sion of Zondervan Publishing House. All
rights reserved.

13 12 11 10 09 08 07 06   9 8 7 6 5 4 3 2 1
0-7847-1899-7

Contents

Introduction

Why talk with your teen about media?

It's no secret that parent-teen relations are often strained. That's what happens when the kids we've loved since the moment we found out they were on their way start to grow from dependent children to independent adults. In today's rapidly changing world, a great deal of parent and teen tension exists over the media choices our teens face and make. Studies consistently show that at times today's media goes over the top with content promoting dangerous and immoral values, attitudes, and behaviors. Parents who monitor their teen's media diet are often alarmed by the content—especially when they realize the powerful role media plays in shaping how their teen looks at and lives life.

It might not seem easy, but part of our parental responsibility is to impart wisdom and advice to help our teens make positive, healthy media choices. When they were younger, we made media choices *for* them. Now that they've entered the teen years and are developing new thinking capabilities, we should be making media choices *with* them. By doing so, we equip them to move on to the independence of adulthood with the ability to live out God-honoring media habits as they make media decisions for themselves.

This book is designed as a practical and informative guide to help you walk with your teen through the confusing maze of today's media world, exploring media sources such as music, videos, TV, movies, video games, computers, and the Internet. As you work through this book and engage your teen in discussions about media, remember that this isn't a "once-and-done" thing. Instead, it's a process. I trust that you and your teen will enjoy this necessary and life-shaping journey.

Walt Mueller

Where Do You Stand?

Working toward helping your teen learn about media and how its various forms affect his life is an important part of parenting. The following questionnaire will help you evaluate your own strengths and weaknesses and where your own values and philosophies fit in. Circle the number that best corresponds to your answer. Then add up the total and check out the How You Scored box. (Consider taking this quiz again after reading the book to see if your score has changed!)

OPTIONS

❶ Strongly agree

❷ Agree somewhat

❸ Disagree somewhat

❹ Strongly disagree

I USE THE INTERNET OR TV ONLY A SHORT AMOUNT OF TIME EACH DAY.

❶   ❷   ❸   ❹

I'D MUCH RATHER SPEND TIME WITH MY TEEN THAN ESCAPE INTO TV, MUSIC, OR THE NET.

❶   ❷   ❸   ❹

I BELIEVE MEDIA CAN BE BOTH A BLESSING AND A CURSE FOR FAMILIES, PEOPLE, AND SOCIETY.

❶   ❷   ❸   ❹

I BELIEVE THAT I CONTROL MY MEDIA CHOICES—THAT THEY DON'T HAVE CONTROL OVER ME.

❶   ❷   ❸   ❹

I BELIEVE THAT TEENS DON'T NEED TVS OR COMPUTERS TO USE IN PRIVATE.

❶ ❷ ❸ ❹

I ENJOY DISCUSSING THEMES OF MOVIES, SHOWS, OR SONGS WITH MY TEEN.

❶ ❷ ❸ ❹

I DISCUSS COMMERCIALS WITH MY TEEN SO SHE DOESN'T BUY INTO EVERY ADVERTISING PROMISE.

❶ ❷ ❸ ❹

I OFTEN CHECK THE LYRICS OF SONGS ON CDS THAT MY TEEN LISTENS TO OR PURCHASES.

❶ ❷ ❸ ❹

I CHECK OFTEN TO SEE IF MY TEEN IS VISITING BLOGS OR OTHER QUESTIONABLE INTERNET SITES.

❶ ❷ ❸ ❹

WE MAKE TIME TO SHARE AS A FAMILY—WITHOUT MEDIA OR ELECTRONICS.

❶ ❷ ❸ ❹

HOW YOU SCORED

10—20 Give yourself a pat on the back! You seem well informed about the different aspects of media and how it affects your teen. You're careful about song lyrics and other media content and look for ways to communicate with and draw near to your family without simply escaping into unhealthy media habits.

21—31 You have a good idea that media is everywhere but may feel a bit helpless to guide your teen into making healthy choices about how long he plays video games or how much music your daughter listens to each day. Take time to chat with your teen about his or her media choices and how they affect lifestyles, values, and time management.

32—40 You probably enjoy TV, videos, and the Internet—but maybe a bit too much! Focus in on what messages about media you're giving your teen as you work toward "media moderation" for both of you!

Media & Teenagers

Teenagers love their media! If you don't believe that, just try taking it away from them sometime. You're bound to have a fight on your hands. In today's world, media is a centerpiece of teenage life and is also a primary influence on how kids think, talk, and act.

Media is pervasive.

Any serious effort to understand and guide our teens through the developmental period of adolescence requires an ongoing effort to understand media and the role it plays in their lives. It's no easy task, especially as media options develop and emerge on a nearly daily basis.

A teen's world is saturated with media.

Your teen's grandparents most likely lived their adolescent years in a world that included a family radio, a record player (or Victrola!), and maybe a television set. Listening and viewing options were limited to a handful of broadcast stations and the vinyl recordings a family could afford. While televisions were in about 87 percent of homes at the end of the 1950s, there were no cell phones, personal computers, video games, or MP3 players. Because media outlets and options were few, families would typically decide together what to watch or listen to in the home.

key point
MEDIA FILLS TEENS' LIVES.

The media world of today's teen is markedly different! A growing array of media outlets and options keeps teens in touch with media and media in touch with them 24-7, no matter where they are or what they're doing. It fills their senses at home, school, work, sporting events, shopping malls, or the car. Many carry portable media devices with them wherever they go.

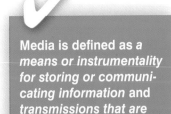

Media is defined as *a means or instrumentality for storing or communicating information* and *transmissions that are disseminated widely to the public.*

For the most part, teens use and interact with media without parental supervision or input. Because outlets and options are so many, it's important we keep in touch with our teenagers' particular media interests and uses. We must know not only where they're spending media time but what they're seeing, hearing, and doing while there, so that we can affirm the good lessons—and challenge the bad.

HOT TOPIC STARTER

How well do you and your teen know each other's media world? Parents, make a list of media types you used as a teen. Have your teen do the same. Discuss what you think is on each other's lists and compare the changes in each other's media worlds.

But monitoring their media isn't enough. Since they are growing up in a media-saturated and media-driven world, we must equip them to interact with and engage media in healthy ways. Rather than thinking about media's messages *for* them, we must think *with* them so they're equipped to make healthy media choices themselves. Wise parents will take the time and effort to understand their teen's media-saturated life and teach the skills needed for their teen to carefully find his way through the media maze.

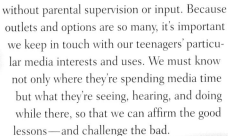

TRY THIS!

Take the National Institutes on Media quiz to see what kind of media habits your family is practicing. You can find it at www.mediafamily.org/facts/mediameasure.asp.

Media is at teens' fingertips.

While teenagers still use traditional "old" media forms (television, radio, movies, magazines), they are using them in new ways. TV remote controls allow teens to channel-surf through seemingly endless options brought into their homes through cable and satellite technologies. Anytime is show time as movies can be viewed at home, on the road, through computers, and even on cell phones. What used to be an entire record collection can be digitally downloaded into a portable listening device the size of a credit card or pen!

"These kids are spending the equivalent of a full-time work week using media, plus overtime. Anything that takes up that much space in their lives certainly deserves our full attention."
—Vicky Rideout (Kaiser Family Foundation)

New media technologies have facilitated changes in where and how teens are listening and watching. At home, floor plans are developed to incorporate state-of-the-art televisions and entertainment centers—and not to just one room in the house. The number of 8- to 18-year-olds with media access in their bedrooms is staggering!

TRY THIS!

Consider doing a home media inventory to see how much media you use at home!

✔ television sets
✔ stereo systems
✔ MP3 players, iPods
✔ video game systems
✔ computers
✔ Internet access
✔ DVD players, VCRs
✔ cell phones

✦ 68% **have a TV**
✦ 37% **have cable or satellite TV**
✦ 54% **have a VCR/DVD**
✦ 10% **have a DVD**
✦ 84% **have a radio**
✦ 86% **have a CD or tape player**
✦ 49% **have a video game player**
✦ 31% **have a computer**
✦ 40% **have a telephone**
✦ 20% **have Internet access**

key point

MEDIA CHANGES HOW TEENS LIVE.

More media options and availability means more media use. In 1999, the total amount of media content young people (ages 8 to 18) were exposed to each day was 7 hours and 29 minutes. Just five years later that amount had increased to 8 hours and 33 minutes a day! Compare that to the time young people spend with their parents (only about 2 hours a day), engaged in physical activity (an hour and a half), doing homework (less than an hour), and performing chores (about a half hour).

Ask your teen to keep a log of his media use this week. Log your media use as well. Compare and discuss your lists at the end of the week.

Average time 8- to 18-year-olds spend per day with media ...

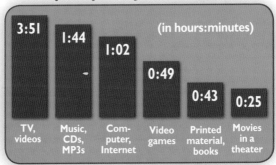

(in hours:minutes)

3:51 — TV, videos
1:44 — Music, CDs, MP3s
1:02 — Computer, Internet
0:49 — Video games
0:43 — Printed material, books
0:25 — Movies in a theater

(Kaiser Family Foundation Report)

All this media technology has changed the face of the world and how teens live in it. Teens worldwide can now interact with each other in real time thanks to instant messaging, cell phones, and other new technologies. They use it to shop, communicate, be entertained, and learn. Media is not only at their fingertips; it's woven in and through the fabric of who they are.

BIG BIBLE POINT

Proverbs 13:20 offers wise advice about the company we keep. Read this verse with your teen and discuss how these truths apply to the media "company" we keep as well. Do our media choices promote wisdom or harm?

Teens are media savvy, yet media illiterate.

Because they've grown up in a world full of media options, teenagers are exceptionally good at learning and using all the different technologies. But that practical skill rarely translates into how to interact mindfully with media.

They can use it all—at once!

It used to be that kids who liked doing their homework with media background noise had two options: (1) do homework in front of the family TV, or (2) go to their room and hit the books with the radio or stereo playing. Because most parents believed it was impossible for kids to concentrate without peace and quiet, they told their kids, "Turn that thing off and do your homework!" Oh, how things have changed!

It's not only important to monitor your teen's media content; it's also important to monitor her media time. If grades are going down while media time is going up, intervene and set media-use limits and parameters.

Today's teens are the consummate media multitaskers, doing their homework while consuming a variety of media all at the same time. In fact, 30 percent of young people say they either talk on the phone, instant message, watch TV, listen to music, or surf the Net most of the time they're doing homework.

✓ MIDDLE-SCHOOL MEMOS

The earlier you establish limits on media use, the easier they are to enforce. Preventive medicine is good. Make and enforce rules while your teen is still young.

Even when the homework's done, teens spend over a fourth of their media time using more than one medium (chatting on a cell phone while instant messaging, reading a magazine while watching TV). Interestingly enough, girls are more prone to multitask than boys. In addition to multitasking, today's teens are able to control and personalize their media use, choosing the options they like by managing individualized playlists and menus, by "surfing" channels and stations, or by instantly switching attention from one form of media to another.

Ask yourself these questions to establish limits on your teen's media multitasking:

Where is homework done?

What media options are in that room?

Does my teen multitask during homework?

What effect has there been on grades?

What "lessons" are being learned from the media?

Do the lessons match what's being taught at home?

Because of their ability to multitask, teens are able to squeeze more media content into smaller amounts of time. Early research is pointing to the fact that their brains are adapting, allowing teens to process multiple streams of information at once. In other words, it's possible they might be telling the truth when they say they can do their homework while media multitasking at the same time.

Just because they can use it all at once doesn't mean it's a good thing.

Mindless media consumption is typical.

Think for a moment about how you and your teenager approach the world of media. There are two basic ways to engage media. Most take the "consume it" approach—watching and listening to anything and everything without thinking consciously or critically about the messages, values, attitudes, and behaviors promoted. This approach, which could also be called *mindless consumption,* assumes that media is nothing more than harmless, neutral entertainment.

key point
ENGAGE MEDIA MINDFULLY.

key point
MEDIA ALWAYS SENDS MESSAGES.

Watch a movie or television show with your teen. Then discuss the messages promoted, deciding whether they're positive or negative based on God's standards.

But media does more than just entertain. Media is a powerful teacher! When we consume media without consciously thinking about it, the messages powerfully shape the way we think, talk, and act—usually without us even realizing it. Teens are especially vulnerable because of where they are in the development process. It's important to remember that media is never neutral. Someone has constructed the media and its message. If we only consume media without thinking about it, messages can have a greater influence on who we are and how we live our lives.

Do you *consume* or *critique* your media choices? Think about it!

> **What is "media literacy"?**
> It's the ability to thoughtfully and deliberately examine and evaluate media, with the end result being wise media choices. Christians practice media literacy based on the unchanging truths of God's Word.

Wise media consumers, both young and old, realize media's power.

They take the *mindful-critique* approach by making a conscious decision to go deeper by listening and watching carefully and critically. Instead of mindlessly allowing media to shape their values, attitudes, and behaviors, they mindfully engage the media by viewing and listening "between the lines" to understand the media's messages. Over time, it becomes second nature to discover media's subtle embedded messages about who and what is important.

BIG BIBLE POINT

In I Corinthians 10:31 the apostle Paul offers a standard that should guide all our actions, including how we interact with media: *"So whether you eat or drink or whatever you do, do it all for the glory of God."*

"Man becomes what he thinks about all day long."
—Ralph W. Emerson

Choose and use media wisely!

By modeling and using mindful critiques, we can teach our teens to look for and find the media's messages. They will learn how to discern both positive and negative aspects of media and become less vulnerable to media's adverse effects on who they are and how they live. This approach equips kids to *control* the media, rather than letting the media control them!

Percent of American homes with a TV

Year	Percent
1950	~8
1960	~85
2004	100

Media can be both positive and negative.

Media is everywhere, shaping our world and guiding us, our children, and our teens. While it can serve as a positive and productive force in society, it is equally effective as a negative, destructive force. Like everything else, it has a good side and a bad side.

Embrace the bright side of media.

Media technology and content expands the world of our teenagers by taking them to the corners of the globe and allowing them to communicate with people near and far. Their exposure to new people, places, and things allows them to see the wonder, glory, and complexity of God's created order. By experiencing new cultures, teenagers are opened up to the rich and wonderful diversity of God's world.

key point
MEDIA CAN BE POSITIVE.

TRY THIS!

Ask your teen to help you create a family website. Use the site as a way to keep faraway relatives and friends updated on family news and happenings.

Media is an educational tool that allows teens to learn about anything!

As an educational tool, media and its nearly limitless nature allows kids to learn about anything and everything. A simple Internet search yields a wealth of information on people, places, or things that teens can use for school projects or to satisfy their interests and curiosities. Playing video or computer games can stimulate curiosity and help teens develop problem-solving skills. Mastering, fixing, or creating a media technology is not only a useful skill but could develop into a vocational calling.

In many ways, society has advanced and improved as a result of the recent media explosion. Communication is lightening-fast, and technology allows us to send our voices, documents, digital files, music, pictures, and e-mails anywhere in the world. Sharing needs creates opportunities to solicit compassion and other resources needed to address social problems near and far. Internet websites can be used to post writings, music, and other information that encourages visitors to consider godly values and God's purpose for life.

TARGET MOMENT

Because many teens believe that adults see little or no good in teen media, go out of your way to look for and comment on messages and portrayals in their media that are positive and God-honoring.

key point

MEDIA CAN SPREAD THE GOOD NEWS.

Watch the evening news or read the newspaper with your teen to discover an area of need in the world. Conduct an Internet search to learn more about that place and its specific needs. Then develop a service project that generates physical or financial help to address the problem.

Take advantage of modern technologies by using media as a tool to foster closeness with your teen. Share a favorite show or movie, listen to music, watch a concert, surf the Internet to explore shared interests, or cheer for a favorite team. God wants us to enjoy the company of each other as we are entertained by media that reflects his will and way for his world.

Media is a powerful tool for breaking down social barriers and building God's kingdom.

Realize that media has a darker side.

Like everything else in our sinful and fallen world, media is not always used in ways that honor and glorify God. Media used in negative ways can promote dangerous messages, and its use can foster harmful results. Media's dark side is more likely to impact teenagers when parents don't monitor and regulate a teenager's media use.

DID YOU KNOW THAT ...

According to one study, 20% of today's video games contain violence against women.

IT'S A PROBLEM OF PERCEPTION!

40%	53%	78%
9- to 10-year-olds	13-year-olds	17-year-olds

Many young girls are unhappy with their bodies when compared to the images they see in the media. What messages are our kids getting as they grow older? –*USA Today* (1996)

Spending too much time with TV has been linked to obesity and a decline in academic performance. Sitting around to listen, play, and watch excessive amounts of media is not only a waste of time but can also lead to lethargy, laziness, and a lack of creativity. Teens immersed in today's media world spend less time playing outside and interacting with others in social situations—patterns that can retard social development and endanger health.

STOP & CONSIDER

Limit the media sources at home to one central room where your family can watch and listen *together*. Outside of clock radios and phones, keep all bedrooms "media-free."

Evidence suggests that media violence promotes aggressive behavior. The constant barrage of sexual references and images may lead teens to engage in immoral sexual behaviors more frequently and at younger ages. Other images and messages glamorize smoking, alcohol, illicit drugs, and unattainable standards of beauty and body type that may contribute to eating disorders, steroid abuse, depression, and treating women as objects.

The National Institute on Media and the Family offers these suggestions on promoting cyber safety with your teen:

- Use blocking or filtering software.
- Establish rules about Internet use.
- Make it a rule not to give out personal information without parental consent.

(Source: www.mediafamily.org)

Obesity is rapidly becoming the most-addressed childhood health problem in today's world. Over the course of the last twenty years, the prevalence of obesity in adolescents has tripled. Is your teenager spending too much time with media, as opposed to spending time in what used to be normal teenage physical activity? (Source: *American Journal of Public Health*, 2004)

While the Internet has brought the wonder of God's world into our homes in new and exciting ways, it is also misused. Pornographic websites are easily accessed, leaving teens with distorted views of sexuality that can affect them for life. Many create fantasized versions of themselves to live out in cyberspace. The Internet is also a place where predators lurk.

MEDIA CAN BE BOTH POSITIVE AND NEGATIVE.

Media's Facets & Forms

More than any previous generation, today's teenagers are surrounded by media outlets and options. As those outlets and options increase in number and sophistication, you can expect your teen's media consumption to grow, along with your need to help your teen manage media in God-honoring ways.

Teens listen to media.

While the days of the old family radio are long gone, teens still spend large amounts of time listening to media every day. Most parents don't know what their teens are listening to, since it's usually done privately through headphones, behind closed doors, or in their cars.

Music is the soundtrack of teen life.

Popular music is everywhere—radio, TV, the Internet, CDs, movie soundtracks, commercials, and at sporting events. Most teens have a CD collection, a stereo in their rooms, and a portable personal stereo with headphones. With music such a big part of teen life, the music industry is always discovering and developing new artists in an effort to gain teens' attention—and money!

Whether positive or negative, the lyrics of today's music speak loud and clear to a generation listening for answers!

In today's world, teenagers can both listen to and watch music. With the advent of MTV, music's connection with kids and the ability to shape their lives increased. Music interprets and defines life by shaping beliefs and providing examples of behavior. The attractive addition of the visual component helps to clarify the meaning of the song. Music videos add sights to the music's sounds, creating a musical package that's far more powerful and influential than simply hearing a song.

One recent study found that 73% of boys and 78% of girls ages 12 to 19 watch MTV, "and it is profoundly influential in the lives of its young fans by glamorizing drug and alcohol use, sexual promiscuity, and violent behavior." (Parents Television Council)

Time teens spend each day listening to tapes, CDs, and MP3s:

11- to 14-year-olds: 45 minutes

15- to 18-year-olds: 1 hour, 9 minutes

(Kaiser Family Foundation)

Kids use the Internet and new digital technologies to access a seemingly endless amount of popular music. They are downloading and copying music to make and manage their own musical playlists that cater to their interests and moods. We need to be diligent in keeping informed as to what music our kids like and the lessons that music teaches them about life.

MIDDLE-SCHOOL MEMOS

As your young teen develops a growing interest in popular music, be sure you listen with him regularly. Then discuss the power of music, the themes and messages of the music, and how to make good music choices. Don't be afraid to say no to music that doesn't meet your standards!

Teens with tape players, CDs, or MP3s in their bedrooms:

11- to 14-year-olds: 89%

15- to 18-year-olds: 92%

(Kaiser Family Foundation)

Teens' radios are usually on!

key point
TODAY'S TEENS ARE TUNING IN TO RADIO.

Radio is a media outlet used heavily by teens, with over 99 percent listening to the radio every week and over 80 percent listening every day. While radio, like other media outlets, has the potential to be a positive, uplifting force in the life of a teen, a casual survey of the most-listened-to radio stations and program formats indicates that radio has become increasingly negative as our moral landscape has changed.

key point
RADIO CONTENT HAS DECLINED.

By far, stations that play around-the-clock contemporary hit music are the stations most teens prefer. Some kids choose to listen to other radio stations that play alternative, country or urban-music formats. Internet and satellite radio are also growing in popularity. These technologies are most popular among older teens, allowing them to further narrow and personalize their listening preferences.

TARGET MOMENT

A simple Google search will help locate song lyrics. Go to www.google.com, then type in the name of the band or the song title, followed by the word "lyrics."

With 91% of 15- to 18-year-olds having a radio in their rooms, more teens are tuning in to music and talk shows. Check out how many hours teens are tuning in!

Girls 12-17: 15 hours
Guys 12-17: 11 hours, 45 minutes

(Radio Today, 2004)

Parents, know the world of radio to be better equipped to lead your child into a spiritually healthy adulthood.

Teenagers who listen to conventional broadcast radio do most of their listening in the morning while getting ready for school, in the evening while doing homework or before going to bed, and on weekends. They also listen while in the car. Because they want to keep their young audience, these stations hire disc jockeys and other personalities who fill the time between songs with advertisements, commentary, banter, contests, and jokes—all geared toward teens. Often this "filler" is offensive, explicit, and inappropriate.

The Center on Alcohol Marketing and Youth discovered the following about the alcohol industry and their placement of radio ads in youth formats:

Alcohol ads were intentionally placed on stations with "youth" formats.

There were more radio ads for beer, "malternatives," and distilled spirits than in adult programs.

Alcohol ads typically aired when youth listened the most.

Youth in African American and Hispanic communities were exposed more than others.

To access music reviews and link to music-review sites, visit the Center for Parent/Youth Understanding website at www.cpyu.org.

Parents should know their teen's radio preferences and take the time to listen in. By doing so, you'll discover how these stations program to teenagers. Take time to talk with your teen, praising the good content and challenging the bad. Always discuss the "why" behind your conclusions. Teach media-evaluation skills that will help your teen make good choices now and for the rest of his life.

Teens watch media.

Visual electronic media is a big part of teens' lives. Television viewing options are growing all the time. Movies are no longer limited to the big screen. Teens can now watch anything and everything in the comfort of their own homes and rooms—or just about anywhere else they choose.

Teens love to watch television.

The average American household is tuned in to television for over 8 hours each day, according to Nielsen Media Research. Kids ages 11-14 watch 3 hours and 16 minutes a day, while those 15-18 watch 2 hours and 36 minutes a day. Combine this with the fact that most parents have made no rules for teens and TV nor have any idea what their teens are watching, and it can become a deadly mix.

7 of 10 teens have TV sets in their bedrooms!

Teens are especially vulnerable and receptive to TV's messages. TV teaches them how to resolve problems and relate to others, what to wear, how to talk, and how to love. "Reality" TV shows are only portrayals of the "reality" producers want to portray. Dangerously, teens rarely recognize this!

Keep TV (and computers) out of your teenager's bedroom. You can't monitor or discuss what your teen is watching when she's alone in her room.

CHECK THIS OUT!

28% of teens 13 to 16 who are reality-show fans said sexuality was the main motivation behind their clothing purchases!

One area where television teaches teens lessons about "real" life is sexuality. Studies show that teens who watch larger amounts of sexual content on television (both depicted sex and discussions of sex) are more likely to engage in intercourse and other sexual activities before those who watch little or no TV sex. Parents should both limit a teen's exposure to sex on TV and talk openly about God's standards for his wonderful gift of sexuality.

Sit down with your teen and see if you can each guess the other's favorite TV show, then watch both shows. Discuss messages and themes in each and God's perspective on them. What issues conformed to or strayed from God's standards of truth?

70% of all shows and 77% of prime-time shows include some sexual content. These shows average 5 sexual scenes per hour.
(Kaiser Family Foundation, 2005)

With cable and satellite television growing in popularity among teens, parents should be concerned about the TV options their kids are choosing. It's vital to find out what they're watching and what they're learning as they watch. While it's important to set limits on your teen's television viewing, it's also important for you to take time to watch with him. Every shared TV experience becomes a teachable moment in which to share God's truth on the issues raised in the show.

Avoid the temptation to have the TV on during dinner. Use that time to catch up, to discuss your day, and to focus on each other.

CHAPTER 2 — MEDIA'S FACETS & FORMS

Teens love movies!

key point
TEACH TEENS TO EVALUATE MOVIES.

Teens are drawn to film because they love stories, they love to be entertained, and they love to escape from the difficulties of their world. Today's movies have even more technical brilliance, special effects, and "star power." On an average day, most teens spend about at least an hour watching DVDs and videos at home—and many also go to movie theaters daily!

Don't underestimate the power of film as a shaper of your teen's values, attitudes, and behaviors. Movie producers know films that address a teen's search for identity, desire for intimacy, and quest for social acceptance will sell because they speak to the deep questions facing kids. For this reason, films have the power to communicate truth or lies about the nature of God's world and how he intends us to live in it.

Getting together with friends to watch a movie is a popular pastime.

If you want to go deeper with your teen by discussing a film's themes as they relate to spirituality, visit www.hollywoodjesus.com or www.ransomfellowship.org.

STOP & CONSIDER

As your teen matures, invite him to help choose appropriate movies. Making choices together teaches discernment and independent thinking.

When helping your teen evaluate a movie, it's not always good to trust the ratings. While ratings may be helpful in discerning content, they don't say anything at all about *context*. There might be an R-rated film that presents ugly truth about life in God's world that needs to be told. Or there might be a "feel-good" PG-rated film that's void of violence, sex, and profanity but makes erroneous assumptions about life.

Studies show that teens who view on-screen violence, smoking, drinking, drug use, and sex are more likely to engage in those behaviors themselves. Guide your teen's choices and encourage him to make wise movie choices himself!

> **When people were asked about movies, nearly half said that viewing movies is one of their two or three favorite types of entertainment.**
> —The Barna Group

key point
MOVIES CAN DISTORT REALITY!

The movie industry fills the eyes and ears of teens in engaging and entertaining ways with the invitation to "come, follow, and experience life." Will you raise your awareness of the world of film and prepare yourself to guard the hearts and minds of your teen? Will you teach and equip her to evaluate and make good movie choices on her own? The key is to ask good questions while watching with careful discernment—a skill our teens need to learn!

Teens read media.

Contrary to what many might think, teens still spend time reading. Even though visual and sound media have become more and more pervasive, teenagers still read print media, particularly magazines and books.

Magazines are more popular than you think!

A trip to the magazine rack at the local bookstore offers proof that teens are buying, reading, and sharing a growing number of attractive and glossy publications published just for them. Because teens aspire to feel, be seen, and be treated as older than they really are, they tend to "read up." For that reason, magazines that appear to be targeting older teen girls are actually being read by girls much younger.

key point
MAGAZINES PROMOTE LIFE STANDARDS.

BIG BIBLE POINT

Read 1 Samuel 16:7 with your teen and then discuss these questions:

- What is more important to God: one's appearance or one's heart? Explain.

- According to teen magazines, what is most important: one's appearance or one's heart? Explain.

- How can we focus on what's really important?

28
Number of minutes the average 11- to 18-year-old spends reading magazines every day.

Teenage girls typically read magazines filled with ads (which usually make up at least half of the content) and articles that deal with fashion, hair and makeup tips, fitness, friendships, and romantic relationships. In recent years, these magazines have added more spiritual content, with a focus on astrology and horoscopes. Covers feature current celebrities whose looks and personalities function as role models for impressionable young readers.

Teenage boys are drawn to magazines that speak to a specific hobby or interest (snowboarding, skateboarding, motorcycles, sports, music) and to the growing number of men's magazines that feature scantily clad females on the cover. The editorial content of these lusty men's magazines usually deals with fashion, sports, gadgets, sexuality, and other "manly" pursuits.

Reading magazines often correlates with body dissatisfaction for women, girls, and even boys. (National Institute on Media and the Family)

Borrow one of your teen's magazines and "deconstruct" it from cover to cover by paying careful attention to the photos, ads, headlines, and article content. What does this magazine tell you about today's teenagers? Once you're done, discuss with your teen what you've discovered in light of God's Word, pointing out areas of agreement and disagreement.

Magazines set standards for teens in relation to fashion, body image, relationships, and spirituality. Covers, ads, and content dictate to our teens the image and character that they think will make them valuable, lovable, and worthwhile.

70%–80% of the people in the U.S. read newspapers and magazines every month.

Magazines have the power to promote and "normalize" standards that are anything but godly.

Yes, teens still read books.

Reading builds knowledge, sparks creativity and imagination, and is good for the development of the brain. While many teens might complain about the amount of reading they're required to do in school, the good news is that many are opting to read books of their own choosing when they're not in school.

key point
ENCOURAGE YOUR TEEN TO READ.

Teens are attracted to books that speak to their interests or needs. Many girls enjoy books about romance and relationships. Boys like books about adventure, sports, and science fiction. It's important to know your teen's reading interests, to ask about what he's reading, and to discuss insight from God's Word on the subjects of his books.

TARGET MOMENT

Choose a book that you and your teen would like to read simultaneously. After reading it, discuss the ideas, messages, and worldview of the author and his or her writing.

AVERAGE TIME EACH DAY TEENS SPEND READING BOOKS

21 minutes
11- to 14-year-olds

24 minutes
15- to 18-year-olds

(Generation M: Kaiser Family Foundation)

Interestingly enough, kids who spend the most time watching TV don't spend any less time reading than other kids do. Kids who spend a greater amount of time playing video games actually spend more time reading than those kids who play fewer video games! But kids do read less when they have a TV in their bedroom, live in homes where the TV is left on all the time, or have parents who haven't established rules about TV watching.

Be sure your teen has a library card.

Give gift cards to bookstores.

Share dessert and browsing in a local bookstore.

Encourage reading classics.

Set limits on media use to encourage reading.

While there's nothing wrong with reading and being entertained by a good story that causes us to think, bookstores are filled with lusty fluff that serves no redeeming purpose. Many romance novels are nothing but gratuitous sex and romance. Many of these books promote the dangerous message that fornication and adultery bring happiness and fulfillment. Remember, your kids are watching what you read! Are you providing a model of wise and God-honoring reading?

Reading is healthy if the material is positive. If your teen gets "lost" in books, work to discover if it's because of a love for books or if it's a way to escape that needs to be addressed. It's important to encourage your teen to read—and to read widely and critically. As with all other media, teach your teen to discern between right and wrong in what she reads by comparing messages and ideas with the truths of God's Word.

Evaluate all books by "The Book."

Teens use interactive media.

Our media-savvy teens have been born into a brave, new digital world where they've mastered electronic technologies we never dreamed possible. Their virtual world is full of wonderful technologies that can be both incredibly good—and extremely dangerous.

Teens play video games.

Video games have come a long way since "Pong" in 1972. Many of the games help teens develop motor skills, hand-eye coordination, and problem-solving abilities. Video games with positive content can be fun to play with family and friends. But the National Institute on Media and the Family, publishers of the annual MediaWise Video and Computer Game Report Card, says that *"every child who plays video games is undergoing a powerful developmental experiment, the results of which we do not yet fully comprehend."*

BIG BIBLE POINT

Engage your teen in reading the Ten Commandments (Exodus 20:1-17). Then evaluate the content of each of his video games in light of these standards. Work to establish personalized video-game standards based on God's will and way as established in the Ten Commandments.

87% of 8- to 17-year-olds play video games at home.

What is known is that more and more teens are entertaining themselves with games that continually push the content envelope. Many games feature interactive violence, profanity, sexual behavior, glorification of drug use, cop-killing, and treating women as objects—all in an effort to accumulate points and "win."

Violent video games rank among the most popular and best-selling titles. It should come as no surprise that behavior practiced and learned in these games can spill out of the virtual world and into the real lives of impressionable teens. "Killology" expert Dr. David Grossman has discovered that kids playing violent video games are submitted to the same repetitive training techniques employed by the military to train soldiers to kill with precision, speed, and efficiency.

CHECK THIS OUT!

"As the graphics of video games in general get more realistic, the danger of them eliciting aggression in the consumer would be greater. When you are exposed to violence like you are in video games where kids and others play them for so many hours at a time, that desensitizes you to what you are seeing."
—Dr. Karen Hill-Scott

Does your teen play video games? If so, how much does she play, what games does she enjoy, and what lessons is she learning while playing? To make sure your teen's gaming experience is positive and healthy, limit video-game time, monitor game purchases, keep game systems out of bedrooms—and take the time to get in on the fun by playing with your teen!

Teen girls and women are the fastest-growing segment of video gaming! They usually opt for relationship video games instead of violence or sports.

Teens spend time online.

Back in 1983, computers were found in only 7 percent of American households. In today's world, almost 9 out of 10 teens live in a home where there's at least one computer. Computers are wonderful tools kids use to learn, communicate, play games, and shop. The Internet has revolutionized how kids communicate as they use e-mail, instant messages, and text-messaging.

The Internet allows anyone to post or access almost anything in split-second time!

key point

THE INTERNET IS BOTH GOOD & BAD!

As with everything else in our sinful and fallen world, cyberspace has a dark side. Kids whose parents don't monitor their computer use are more prone to fall into these traps, especially the growing number of teens who use a computer in the privacy of their own bedroom. Just as responsible parents protect their young children from dangers, they should work to be sure their teen's online experience is positive, healthy, and safe.

To learn a step-by-step process for finding and accessing your kid's online diaries, log on to The Center for Parent/Youth Understanding's website at www.cpyu.org.

MIDDLE-SCHOOL MEMOS

Only 23% of today's middle- and high-school students say their parents have set rules about the length of time they spend online and the sites they visit. Only 22% say their parents know where they go online. Do you monitor how your teen spends his or her online time?

PERCENTAGE OF TEENS WHO ...

✦ **Use the Internet – 85%**

✦ **Check e-mail – 82%**

✦ **Instant-message – 52%**

✦ **Read blogs or web journals – 38%**

✦ **Go into chat rooms – 13%**

✦ **Post personal info so others can contact them – 42%**

✦ **Have talked about sex online with someone they've never met – 27%**

✦ **Have talked about meeting someone they've met online – 30%**

(USA Today and Polly Klaas Foundation)

One of the greatest and most alluring dangers of the Internet is the growing number of pornographic websites for guys. Girls struggling with eating disorders can access "pro-anorexia" websites that teach them how to "succeed" and celebrate the goddess known as "Ana." Cyberbullying occurs when kids use the anonymity of the Internet to threaten others.

62% of online teens say they believe most teens do things online they'd rather their parents not see!

A more subtle danger exists around online diaries known as "weblogs" or "blogs." Like the written diaries of days past, teens use these highly personalized sites to express themselves. They not only post personal information, photos, and favorite music but also share their deepest thoughts, joys, questions, and struggles for the world to see. You should check out and monitor your teen's sites on a regular basis in order to know what's happening in his or her life and world.

The largest teen blog site may well be "myspace.com." This site, and other smaller ones, have been linked to predators trolling for teens who give out personal information, nude photos, and more. Warn your teen not to give personal data on these sites!

Media delivers teens to marketers.

Marketing might just be the most pervasive and powerful media force in teenagers' lives. It targets them, more than any other age group, through strategic placement in all media outlets, including TV, movies, the Internet, radio, magazines, and video games.

Advertisers target teens.

You can't go anywhere in today's world without seeing or hearing an ad. Most of advertising exists for one reason: *to deliver the audience to advertisers.* It's possible that teens see more ads than any other age group, since they spend 29 hours a week using traditional media (TV, radio, Internet, magazines, and newspapers), and 32 hours a week in activities that expose them to additional marketing messages (driving, sports events, restaurants, concerts).

The basic premise of advertising to teens is to create a need for products by understanding and

> **Prosperity** knits a man to the **world.** He feels that he is **finding** his place in it, while **really** it is finding its **place** in him.
> —C. S. Lewis (*The Screwtape Letters*)

exploiting teens' anxieties and aspirations. Teens want to feel better, look nicer, and fit in. Advertising manipulates them into thinking that, if they use a certain product, their needs will be met, they will be happy, they'll fit in, and they'll finally be able to enjoy life.

✓ **The average American encounters 3,500 to 5,000 marketing messages a day!**

key point

TEENS CAN BE EXPLOITED BY ADS.

Marketers work hard and spend lots of money to understand and target teens. Why? First, there are currently over 33 million teens in the U.S., as compared to only 18 million just 40 years ago. Second, teens have tremendous spending power. Third, they influence how their parents and friends spend money. Fourth, marketers know that the kids they reach early will be loyal to a brand for the rest of their lives. Finally, kids are more easily influenced than adults because they're more impulsive and susceptible to emotional appeals.

Why market to teens?
- 33 million teens to reach!
- Teens are impulsive!
- Teens have huge spending power!
- Teens build brand loyalty.
- Teens influence parents' spending.

BIG BIBLE POINT

Discuss how Jesus' words in Mark 8:36 relate to advertising: "What good is it for a man to gain the whole world, yet forfeit his soul?"

But advertisements don't just sell products. Their greatest ability is to *shape the beliefs* that drive teenage behavior.

Ads influence the way teens look at, understand, and live their lives. For example, ads can sell the idea that "things bring happiness," that "I deserve it all," or that "if you use this product, you will be sexy; after all, if you aren't sexy, you won't have sex—which everyone else your age is doing." As parents, we must help our teens understand how and why they're targeted, along with an understanding of the many exploitative lies marketers fire their way.

Teach your teen to think critically about ads. Choose an ad, then ask the following:

- What product is this ad selling?
- What else does this ad sell? (ideas, lifestyle, worldview, behaviors, etc.)
- What's the bait, hook, and promise of the ad?
- Is the hook true? Explain.

Advertising works—and here's how.

Why are marketers spending $2,200 a year per U.S. household? Why is the annual marketing budget in the U.S. $278 billion? Why do advertisers spend $2.4 million for a 30-second ad spot during the Super Bowl? And why do researchers tell us that kids are able to recognize brand logos at just 18 months old? The answer is simple: *advertising works.* It's especially effective with our teens.

Teens eat up advertising! They look to ads to let them know if they're dressing right, hanging out with the right friends, and using products that promise instant "cool" appeal!

Parents must take the time to learn about the strategies marketers use to reach teens. They must also help teens see how those strategies are used to manipulate them. "Branding" is the process of grabbing a teen's interest, being adopted by the teen, and becoming a crucial part of his or her daily life. Marketers have branded successfully when their product is not only immediately recognizable but when it is adopted by kids as their identity. The brand becomes who they are and what they stand for.

Researchers tell us that kids are able to recognize brand logos at 18 months old!

When marketers employ the "cool factor," they have gotten kids to identify their product as being most desirable among members of the teenage population. Coolness plays into peer pressure and our teens' need to fit in and not feel left out. Marketers actually infiltrate fringe teen populations to discover and identify the next big trend. Then they steal it, manufacture it, and market it with the hopes of getting it into the hands of the most popular "influencer" teens. In an effort to be cool, the "wannabe" followers will follow the influencers' lead.

TRY THIS!

Tape a TV commercial during a popular teen show. View the ad a few times, then discuss these questions related to advertising strategies:

✦ **What techniques are used to sell this product?**

✦ **How are lighting, angles, focus, and close-ups used?**

✦ **How is music used to manipulate emotions and create moods?**

✦ **What inadequacies, anxieties, and aspirations does this ad exploit or prey on?**

✦ **How does this ad make me try to "need" this product?**

Cool sells—at least to most teens, who are influenced greatly by their peers.

Turn your next car trip into a "marketing field trip." See how many ads you spot. Choose random ads to discuss the techniques marketers use to sell their products.

Advertisers are also effective at exploiting teen yearnings, anxieties, and the drive for independence. They will associate the product with relational connections, positive feelings, fun, a celebrity, or sex appeal—all things that are important to teens.

Media's Powerful Functions

Whether teens realize it or not, what they see, hear, and experience in and through the media influences their values, attitudes, and behaviors. Knowing how media shapes and defines teens' reality increases parents' ability to connect with and guide their teens.

Media is a map to life.

Because they're growing through a change-filled developmental period that leaves them full of questions and searching for direction, teenagers are especially vulnerable to the map media lays out to guide them from the dependence of childhood into the independence of adulthood.

Media shapes teens' worldviews.

key point

TEENS
ARE
SEARCHING
FOR ANSWERS.

Because they're curious and uncertain about life, teenagers are looking for information to help them make sense of the world and how they're to live in it. Media's images and words meet teens where they're at in attractive and relevant ways that capture their attention, engage their emotions, and shape their worldview.

Media offers teens answers to worldview questions such as, *Who am I? Where do I fit in? What is real? Who's in control?* and *How can I recognize right from wrong?*

A worldview is the model, lens, and framework through which we view the world around us, our purposes in life, and our futures. Every teen lives his worldview each day. It's the basis for how teens think and act. Some people consciously choose their worldview, but for most teens theirs is a subconscious collection of answers they've picked up along the way. Much of what they pick up comes from media that communicates information about how to live and react in this world.

> "A worldview describes the way the world is, while also providing a model for the way the world ought to be."
>
> —William Romanowski (*Eyes Wide Open: Looking for God In Popular Culture*)

Christians believe that a Christian worldview is shaped by the truths of God's Word, the Bible.

Research has shown that media exposure affects a broad range of adolescent attitudes and behaviors, including body image, eating disorders, violence, sexuality, and tobacco and alcohol use. Media also teaches powerful lessons about God, love, priorities, and relationships. If teens attend the "school" of media without parental oversight or input, the voice of the media "teacher" will increase in both volume and persuasive capacity. It's important to know where our kids are spending their media time and what they're learning while there. Then we can evaluate these media lessons with our teens under the light—and wisdom—of God's Word.

Media tends to influence gradually over time as kids are repeatedly and cumulatively exposed to similar media portrayals and messages.

Media's power to affect is increasing.

Today's teenagers spend more time with media than any previous generation. They have more media technologies, outlets, and options at their disposal. Many spend a growing amount of time with media while spending a decreased amount of time engaged with families, schools, and churches. As a result, media has become a *primary* source of information for teens on everything from sexuality to politics to alternative lifestyles to issues of right and wrong.

The power of media to define reality and shape worldviews increases daily.

key point
MEDIA'S POWER GROWS DAILY.

key point
PARENTS CAN STILL INFLUENCE TEENS!

BIG BIBLE POINT

Read Deuteronomy 6:4-9. Based on these verses, what are some practical steps you can take to increase your influence on your teen's values, attitudes, and behaviors?

A synthesis of eighteen studies completed in the early 1980s compares the influence of various institutions on the values and behaviors of 13- to 19-year-olds and how this influence has shifted over time. The study showed that in 1960 the family exercised the greatest influence on teen values and behavior. Other institutions of influence, in order, were school, friends and peers, and the church. For the most part, these institutions were in agreement on basic values and matters of right and wrong, thereby providing a relatively unified voice in terms of their influence on teens.

No study or research has ever shown that kids turn on the TV, radio, computer, or MP3 player for the purpose of learning. This does not mean, however, that media won't teach or communicate information. Learning takes place even when learning is not the reason for media use.

By 1980, friends and peers had jumped to number one as the greatest influencer of teen values and behavior. The family dropped to number two, and the media jumped onto the list (think MTV!) at number three. School dropped to fourth, and the church dropped out altogether.

MAJOR INFLUENCES ON
TEENS 13 TO 19 YEARS OLD

1960	1980	2005
1. FAMILY	1. FRIENDS	1. MEDIA
2. SCHOOL	2. FAMILY	2. FRIENDS
3. FRIENDS	3. MEDIA	3. FAMILY
4. CHURCH	4. SCHOOL	4. SCHOOL

What does the list look like today? Because of its overwhelming power and presence, media jumps to the top of the list. Friends and peers, immersed in and influenced by the same media voices, drop to number two. The family, broken down in so many ways by the increase of divorce and the decrease in family time, drops to number three. School stays at number four. But the list doesn't have to look this way in your home. Parental presence in the form of time, love, and attention means that your voice of influence will be heard above the never-ending sound of media voices.

Media creates role models.

Today's teens know more than just media's plot lines, lyrics, and visual images. Tabloid TV, reality shows, Internet fan sites, and celebrity magazines take teens beyond media's surface into the behind-the-scenes world of the lifestyles of their rich and famous heroes. Kids are dressing, acting, thinking like, and being shaped by these celebrities. It's not just the chart-topping music, TV shows, and movies that teach kids. It's also the chart-toppers themselves!

1% — Number of TV shows containing sex that have a primary thematic emphasis on sexual *risks* or *responsibilities* throughout the episode or show

(Kaiser Family Foundation, 2005)

The look of "media celebrities du jour" shapes teen fashion, hairstyles, and behaviors!

Media's role models are trendsetters who shape the styles teenagers covet, purchase, embrace, and wear. Because adolescents look and long for attention and peer acceptance, they model themselves after those icons in the spotlight who have captured the interest of our kids.

TRY THIS!

Make a list of your teen's media role models. Use the Google Internet search engine to find websites, blogs, and fan discussions. Take some time to visit these sites, making notes of what you've learned about the messages these role models send to their vulnerable young followers.

Of the 20 most highly rated shows for teen viewers, only one in ten with sexual content includes a reference to sexual risks or responsibilities at some point in the episode.

(Kaiser Family Foundation, 2005)

Media also creates peer role models by design. Because there's lots of money to made by selling celebrity lifestyles and fashions to teens, marketers work hard to "clothe" the trendsetters in the student population in celebrity style. Marketers know that if this influential group that makes up about 10 percent of the teen population adopts celebrity style, 50 to 80 percent of all teens will follow the lead of these "pied pipers" in an effort to be in style and up to date. It's a powerful formula that's working well.

BIG BIBLE POINT

Read Romans 12:1, 2 with your teen, then discuss the following.

✦ How do these verses relate to your media role models and the values, attitudes, and behaviors they promote?

✦ Do any of today's media role models promote values, attitudes, and behaviors that are contrary to God's will? Explain.

As you discover your teen's media role models, look beyond the surface influences to how these role models influence your teen's heart. Because our current media environment provides access to every detail about stars, teens are easily influenced by the stars' values, attitudes, and behaviors. Their examples shape our teens' views on everything from marriage, sex, and love to spirituality, drug use, and body image.

MIDDLE-SCHOOL MEMOS

We need to encourage and help young teens examine their heroes according to biblical standards. Otherwise, they run the risk of accepting and emulating traits and attitudes that are dangerous and wrong.

Media is a mirror.

Taking the time to get to know your teenager's media is a valuable way to get to know your teenager and his or her world. Stand behind your teen and look into the mirror of his media. Your eyes will be opened to the issues you need to lovingly discuss and address. Knowing media preferences gives us insight into our teens' emotional and spiritual health.

Media reveals the spirit of the age.

The Old Testament includes groups of people who joined King David's army, along with the qualities that made them effective members of David's team. One of these groups was the *"men of Issachar, who understood the times and knew what Israel should do"* (1 Chronicles 12:32). They had great insight into the culture of their world. For that reason, they were able to develop plans of action that addressed the realities and needs of their particular place in history.

key point
MEDIA HELPS US UNDERSTAND OUR TEENS.

Take an honest look at your own media choices. What values do you see reflected in them?

In the same way, wise parents recognize the reflective power of their teenagers' media, develop a working understanding of that media and its messages, then use that understanding to develop responses to guide their teens into emotional and spiritual health. Looking into the mirror of their media helps us to understand the basic values of their world and the worldview they are being taught during their daily media involvement.

Take time to discover your teen's unique media habits and interests, along with the messages the media's sending. These media messages are "true" in the sense that they reflect the worldview, spirit, and beliefs of the culture—even if they deny what God's Word tells us is true. Media is always true in this way, since it's the map that expresses and shapes the reality of our teens. Just because God's truth might be denied or left out of the media's message doesn't mean we should ignore it.

Watch a music video with your teen. Discuss how the visual and lyrical messages reflect how our culture teaches people to think, talk, and act, then list which are in opposition to or agreement with God's will.

It's essential to know your teenager's media. If you want to help your teen grow into an emotionally and spiritually healthy adulthood, you must listen to her media and understand the way this media map is shaping her values, attitudes, and behaviors. Then, and only then, can you understand the times and know how to respond to in a manner that steers your teen away from media's lies and affirms media's truth.

HOT TOPIC STARTER

Jesus said, "Out of the overflow of the heart the mouth speaks" (Matthew 12:34). Discuss with your teen the idea that, just as what artists choose to sing is reflective of who they are, what we listen to can be reflective of who we are. Does your teen agree or disagree and why?

Media reveals teens' concerns and issues.

key point

MEDIA SPEAKS FOR TEENS.

The teenage years are difficult, with many hormonal and social changes. Add the additional pressures today's world throws at kids, and adolescence is that much harder. Teens often turn to media, particularly music, as a way to express their anger (and other emotions) or soothe their pain. Because they often have difficulty putting feelings into words, teens will be drawn to and identify with music and other media that expresses what they're feeling.

Disconnected teens often turn to music groups to express their own anger and frustration—even adopting their styles of dress and language.

This is especially true for the kids who hurt the most. Teenage subcultures are often built around a particular style of music or band that expresses their common experience of pain and brokenness. Disconnected and disenfranchised teens have come together around some of the more extreme music genres, including heavy metal, punk, goth, and thrash. These communities serve as families where kids find belonging. Teens adopt their music, films, clothing styles, and language to define who they are and to separate them from others.

TRY THIS!

Log on to the Center for Parent/Youth Understanding website at www.cpyu. org to read more on why and how many of today's singers and bands are connecting with teenagers.

"Behind music that shocks there are often neglected social and personal issues needing to be explored."
—Dean Borgman, *Implications*

Parents must understand the different types of popular music and media their kids adopt as their own, the unique features of each, and the reasons why kids are drawn to these different styles and types. Teens form genre preferences and allegiances that define who they are in relationship to their families, peers, school, and the broader society.

Who is your favorite singer or band? Why?

What is your favorite song or album? Why?

What has connected you to this music?

Does the music express anything that bothers you?

How can I help with problems in your life that this music addresses?

If you want to know your teenager intimately, you need to stop and listen long and hard to your teen and his media. Music oftentimes puts into words what kids feel but can't express themselves. While your teen's negative music and media preferences won't always be a reflection of deeper struggles and problems, it's important to err on the side of caution by digging deeper, asking questions, and trying to get at the root of the attraction, since media often serves to reveal teens' cares, troubles, issues, and problems.

Think back to your own teenage years and the music you listened to. When you hear that music today, what memories, feelings, and experiences are conjured up? How do they help you identify or understand your teen better?

Media helps us speak with credibility.

Parents can lose credibility with their teens when they pass judgment on media they haven't experienced for themselves!

The symptoms of egg-on-the-face syndrome are easy to spot. A group of Christians or an individual criticizes a film, television show, or rock band as contributing to the moral decline of teens. They levy strong accusations against the "offender" and recruit others to join the crusade. All too often, parents who take this approach act as if they know what they're talking about—but they don't. Why? Because they react on the basis of misinformation they heard second- or third-hand. As soon as they are challenged, they wind up with egg on their faces because they've never seen, heard, or investigated the very thing they're criticizing!

The next time you engage your teen in a discussion about music or media, follow these simple rules to make communication more positive and profitable:

- **Don't act like you have all the answers.**
- **Be sure to listen to your teen.**
- **Ask clarifying questions.**
- **Have the facts straight before disagreeing or defending your view.**
- **Don't get angry. Demonstrate the patience, compassion, and love of Christ!**

If we're going to be responsible in our efforts to help our teens make good media choices, we must prepare ourselves so we know what we are talking about. We can't attack an album, movie, or show on the basis of what we've heard in an extended game of whisper-down-the-lane. We need to know the facts so that we can intelligently discuss the media and messages that concern us.

The Ultimate Band List (www.ubl.com) is a great place to learn about musical genres, artists, and bands. For a list of other helpful sites, see www.cpyu.org/Page.aspx?id=76664

This approach has biblical precedent. When the apostle Paul began discussions with the idolatrous people of ancient Athens, he did so in an informed manner (Acts 17:22, 23). He didn't open his mouth until he knew what he was talking about. This same approach allows us to be better informed, credible in the eyes of our teens, and more effective as communicators of what is right and true. Our teens are more apt to listen to us when we have done our research. It tells them that we care enough about them that we are willing to take the time to know as much as we can about what's important to them.

Here are suggestions to help you stay informed about the world of teen music and media:

Read the entertainment page in your local newspaper.

Browse through your teen's CD collection or computer playlist.

Watch an hour of MTV each week or share a movie with your teen.

Browse through magazines such as *Rolling Stone, Blender,* or *Entertainment Weekly.*

Making Media Choices

As parents entrusted with the nurture and care of our children, we must take positive and productive steps to help them find their way through the maze of today's media. Our approach should equip them to choose and use media in a manner that brings honor and glory to God.

Establish a plan for wise media use.

Before discussing media habits and choices with your teen, take time to deal with some foundational issues that will help you more effectively teach your teen to manage the world of today's media. Come up with a game plan for choosing and using media wisely!

Avoid the extremes of reacting to media.

key point

MEDIA CAN SEND POSITIVE MESSAGES.

We can't deny the potent power of media to manipulate and shape our teens during their adolescence. Faced with this reality, many of us make the mistake of responding to the challenges we've discussed in this book by going to one of two extremes: (1) we avoid media contact, or (2) we ignore the dangers. Both reactions do nothing to help our kids learn for themselves how to watch and listen with discernment.

Don't overreact—or underreact—to media's power!

RUN-FOR-YOUR-LIFE RESPONSE

We should avoid the "run-for-your-life" response. Perhaps media's more negative aspects have tempted you to eliminate the threat and danger by separating your teen from all media. By taking this unrealistic approach, we force our kids to miss out on the opportunity to learn how to make good media decisions for themselves. In addition, eliminating all media keeps our kids from media messages that are positive, good, true, right, and honorable.

I-DIDN'T-HEAR ANYTHING RESPONSE

We should also avoid the "I-didn't-hear-anything" response. We can't casually overlook the power of media to shape the values, attitudes, and behaviors of our teens. Allowing our teens to listen to and watch anything and everything opens the door for media's voices—the good and the bad—to come in and answer the questions that our teens have. Failing to offer guidance and direction is an unrealistic, uncaring, and unloving approach to parenting.

It's important to avoid the mistake of both overestimating and underestimating the power of media in the lives of our teens. *Parental silence* sends the faulty message that our teens can partake of anything without fear of harm. *Prohibiting everything* sends the faulty message that media has no potential for good.

When kids are young, we think *for* them, setting clear limits on their media habits. As they get older, we should think *with* them by discussing how to make good media choices. In this way, we prepare them to think for themselves as enter their adult years.

Help teens rely on God's standards.

Whether you know it or not, all media choices are based on some authority. When it comes to making healthy media choices, what standards should you use to decide what's worth your teen's media time? What standards should you teach your teen to have to help decide what's safe and what's dangerous on the Internet? When it comes to program and lyrical content, how should you and your teen judge what's "good" and what's "bad" in movies or music?

God's Word denotes certain values, qualities, and truths we can use as standards to help make wise media choices.

TRUTH

NOT CAUSING OTHERS TO STUMBLE

HONESTY

SELFLESS SACRIFICE

HONORING GOD

Listening to music is a teen's number one nonschool activity. Check out positive music alternatives that reflect a Christian worldview and help your teen choose music that honors God!

Some parents choose to pass judgment based on personal preference. Others decide what they like and don't like based on what they were raised to believe. Others share whatever convictions their friends have. And many simply follow media's lead, assuming that if a show, song, or film is popular and everyone else is listening or watching it, then it must be good!

But when it comes to evaluating media sources and making positive media choices, we must appeal to a trustworthy, time-tested, and believable authority—not just for our teens, but for ourselves. As Christians, we should use the Bible as the authoritative measuring stick and guide for evaluating everything we see and hear. The difficulty lies in the fact that God never gives direct instruction on particular types of media.

> Making healthy media choices doesn't mean we should avoid all messages that are "ugly" in nature. Remember: ugliness reflects the truth when it offers a clear picture of the way the world is. The Bible is filled with descriptions of ugliness that lead to an understanding of the reality of sin's effects, along with our deep need for the Savior. Brainstorm with your teen about songs, films, or TV shows that reveal the truth about our world's dark, sinful side.

Ephesians 5:1-11
Philippians 4:8

Galatians 5:16-26
Colossians 3:1-17

How can these verses help shape your media choices?

John 17:13-19
Mark 12:28-34

I Thessalonians 4:1-8
Ecclesiastes 12:13, 14

When you look more deeply into God's Word, you'll find specific and helpful guidance on what to enjoy and what to avoid, what's good and what's bad, what is truth and what are lies. We should read the Bible with the deliberate intent of finding guidance for our media habits and choices. We're called to carefully discern and evaluate all media choices in light of God's Word.

Examine your own media choices.

When it comes to media use and choices, what kind of lifestyle and habits are you modeling for your teen? The most effective teaching method is *teaching by example*. We're only fooling ourselves if we think we can say one thing and do another. Children learn from watching how we choose and use media in our own lives. If we are to be effective parents and teachers, our lives must be marked by integrity. In other words, *our behaviors must flow out of our stated beliefs.*

key point

EVALUATE YOUR OWN MEDIA HABITS.

According to the Barna Group, 86% of teens believe that music piracy (copying a CD for a friend or downloading nonpromotional music online for free) is either morally acceptable or not even a moral issue. Only 8% claim that such activity is morally wrong. Among Christian teens, only 10% claim that such activity is morally wrong. What are they learning from your example if you enjoy downloading music?

key point

PARENTAL EXAMPLE IS VERY POWERFUL!

TRY THIS!

Log your media use for one week, recording how much time you spend and what messages you're seeing and hearing. Then evaluate your media habits. How do they reflect—or not reflect—the media habits you want to teach your teen? How can improve your example?

Here are a few difficult questions all parents must ask themselves about their own media use!

1 How much time do I spend in front of the TV or computer?

2 Are there shows I watch only when I'm alone or if my teen is away?

3 Do I laugh at sitcom humor that's racist or sexual or that devalues people?

4 Is it difficult for me to turn off media and spend time with my family?

79% of teens ages 10 to 17 have watched an R-rated movie with their parents on video or in a theater!

Each of us as parents must be sure that we have evaluated and adjusted our own media habits before we begin to deal with our teens' habits. By consistently modeling responsible viewing, listening, and computer behavior, we can become signposts pointing our teens in the right direction. Otherwise, we're phonies—and teens can sniff out phonies very quickly!

Implement media evaluation steps.

A positive approach to helping your teen face the world of media begins with you. There are several steps you can take to teach your teen how to make healthy media choices both now—and for the rest of his or her life.

Discover media's messages.

We must take the time to teach our teens how to deliberately take the step of discovery with every song, film, TV show, or media piece they use. Because of media's ability to shape values, attitudes, and behaviors, we must help our teens discover the messages that media promotes.

key point
ALL MEDIA CONTAINS UNDERLYING MESSAGES.

Discovery is the process of thoughtfully and carefully listening and watching to hear or see the underlying worldview of the media with which you're engaged. It's imperative to dig deep enough to identify the message communicated through the media.

Sometimes media messages come through loud and clear. Other times, it will be a difficult task that requires thought because the message isn't at the surface. Remind your teen that it's always important to take time to engage in the discovery process, since there is always a message in media—whether it's easy to find or not.

key point
WORK TO DISCOVER MEDIA'S MESSAGES!

To make the discovery process more fruitful, gather background information on the media piece. For example, if you're evaluating a song, do an Internet search on the band to find out more about their story and what they sing about. For a TV show, visit the show's website to learn more about plot lines, characters, and previous episodes. This will give you a more balanced sense of who is making the media and what they believe.

As you watch and listen, filter what you see and hear through these questions— questions that will help you and your teen get started on your quest to discover important truths and dangerous inaccuracies or agendas in the underlying message and worldview of the media:

> **What does it say about God?**
> **What does it say about humanity?**
> **Is the one true God replaced by another deity?**
> **What does it say about happiness and where it comes from?**
> **Is it hopeful or hopeless?**
> **What does it say about the nature of sexuality?**
> **Are solutions offered to life's problems? If so, what are they?**

The Center for Media Literacy suggests that parents and teens ask these five "discovery" questions of all media:

1. **Who created this message?**
2. **What techniques are used to attract my attention?**
3. **How might different people understand this message differently from me?**
4. **What lifestyles, values and points of view are represented in, or omitted from, this message?**
5. **Why was this message sent?**

(*Five Key Questions That Can Change the World*, Center for Media Literacy, 2005)

Discern media's messages.

It's important for teens to discern the differences between truth and lies and reality and fantasy. In our world, media has the ability to communicate both truth and lies in entertaining and engaging ways—often at the same time. We frequently become so immersed in being entertained that we never consciously think about how messages that may be false are subtly embedding themselves into who we are, how we think—and what we believe.

key point
MEDIA PROMOTES BOTH TRUTH & LIES.

key point
MEDIA PROMOTES REALITY & FANTASY.

"Let us discern for ourselves what is right; let us learn together what is good" (Job 34:4).

"Sometime, someday, our children will be on their own, trying to live in but not of the world. Will they have the tools they need? Are you helping them to discern between wisdom and foolishness, between truth and lies? Good questions and good character. Together they give our children the skills to negotiate a world where the lies are all dressed to kill."

—Steve Garber (*Don't Leave Your Brains at the Box Office*)

Once you and your teen have discovered the media's message, the next step is to carry out the process of *discernment*. Discernment is the practice of looking more closely at what you've discovered and distinguishing those things God says are good, true, healthy, and right from those things God says are evil, false, dangerous, and wrong.

Evaluate everything you learned in the discovery step against the measuring stick of God's Word in order to determine whether or not there is agreement or disagreement with God's never-changing truth. How do you do this? Take all the questions you asked in the discovery process along with the answers you dis-covered, then compare the media's answers with God's answers to those questions.

DID YOU KNOW THAT...

The average teen spends 4 to 5 hours each day listening to music or watching music videos!

Because of the power media has to shape our teens, we must model and teach discernment skills that will lead them to the point where they are able to recognize and embrace media's truths, while rec-ognizing and rejecting media's lies. Media that communicates truth and reality has the power to move teens toward a deeper love for God and an understanding of his world.

STOP & CONSIDER...

God's message to your teen about media might go like this: *Because I love you, imitate and think about me! Avoid imitating false messages and behaviors I say are wrong. Don't let media pull you away from me and my ways. Prayerfully look at the world of all media through the eyes of my Word.*

Decide how to use media's messages.

Now it's time to take the last media evaluation step by working with your teen to make decisions about the media he or she chooses and uses. There are three levels at which a decision must be made. The first is whether or not to engage and use the media for the purpose of *entertainment.* The second is whether you'll use media for *educational* reasons. And the third is whether or not to engage and use media for its *ministry* value.

key point
MEDIA CREATES CHOICES FOR US.

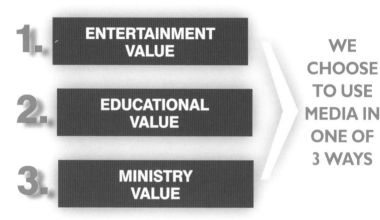

1. **ENTERTAINMENT VALUE**

2. **EDUCATIONAL VALUE**

3. **MINISTRY VALUE**

WE CHOOSE TO USE MEDIA IN ONE OF 3 WAYS

ENTERTAINMENT VALUE

Entertainment decisions can be based on simple criteria. If what is being taught is in agreement with biblical truth and your family's values, then your teen should celebrate and enjoy the media. But if it contradicts his faith, then he needs to decide whether or not this option should be a part of his media diet. Two questions you should teach your teen to ask of all media are: *Should I listen or watch?* and *Will I listen or watch?*

EDUCATIONAL VALUE

Media can entertain and inform your teen, yes—but don't overlook the power of various media sources for their potential to educate. The Internet can expand a teen's knowledge of the world, its people, and common social concepts—as well as worldwide problems, including hunger, war, and poverty. School and studying can be enriched by the Internet, technological magazines, and newspapers. Encourage your teen to look beyond entertainment to discover the many educational choices available through media!

Using media for education and ministry can open teens' eyes to the world's need in amazing ways—and allow them to make a difference!

MINISTRY VALUE

The need for a ministry value decision is a valid consideration for teenagers who are living and growing in their relationship with Christ and moving toward spiritual maturity. They should be trained to engage media with a desire to allow the media to help them understand the world in which they've been called to live out their faith and the people with whom they've been called to share their faith. For more mature teens, media that may be inappropriate for entertainment use can serve to open their eyes to the hurt, pain, and needs in the world.

Media's ministry value can be determined by asking these questions:

> How does this media choice help me understand the needs of my culture and my friends?

> How would Jesus share his message with people who think and live this worldview?

> What examples from Jesus and God's people shape my response to these needs?

Establish healthy media boundaries.

The dictionary defines a boundary as *something that indicates or fixes a limit or extent.* While some resistance should be expected, teenagers need their parents to lovingly explain and set media-use boundaries.

Warn teens of media's dangers.

It's not unusual for conflict to occur whenever a parent steps in to set limits on his or her teen. One of the primary parent and teen battles that takes place during the adolescent years occurs over teens' media choices and use. While teenagers are beginning to think for themselves (and they certainly aren't children any longer), they still don't have fully formed intellectual capabilities. Nor do they have the wisdom

and discernment skills that come with adult experience. Because of our God-given responsibilities as parents, we need to set media-use limits and boundaries.

BIG BIBLE POINT

"Your word is a lamp to my feet and a light for my path" (Psalm 119:105). Discuss how this verse speaks to the need for media boundaries and limits. How does knowing and following God's Word protect us from falling prey to media dangers?

Sadly, one of the biggest problems facing teens today is that many are growing up in families where parents have forfeited their responsibility to set limits. Our kids need us to help them learn how to function responsibly in the world. By providing them with clear-cut boundaries, we offer them the opportunity to make their own choices within the safety of limits—while protecting them from the dangers of unrestricted freedom.

✓ MIDDLE-SCHOOL MEMOS

As your teen grows, he will desire and expect increased independence. Consequently, he is more likely to receive and respect the media limits you set if you set those limits early on. If you're the parent of a middle schooler, take time to set those limits now!

These limits and rules will be received more readily by your teen if you establish them in the context of a loving, patient relationship. It's also important for you to explain that the limits and rules exist for the purpose of protecting your teen from harm and providing for long-term well-being.

Be patient in setting boundaries. Make the limits clear, simple, and logical. Go over the consequences for infractions—then be consistent in enforcing your limits!

Take time to explain that, while media offers great benefits, there are also a variety of dangers that exist. Talk to your teen about the emotional and physical dangers that exist, including everything from cyberbullying to lack of exercise and obesity. Explain the social dangers that arise, from separating oneself from healthy interaction with others to learning inappropriate ways of resolving conflicts. And don't forget to mention the spiritual dangers of assimilating ideas that are contrary to your values.

1 in 17
kids has been cyber-bullied!

Cyber-bullying occurs when a person is threatened or harassed by another person online. Report threats and severe bullying to your service provider or the police.

Set boundaries on time.

It's no secret that teens are spending a growing amount of time utilizing the ever-increasing media options at their disposal. Spending too much time with media increases media's ability to influence and shape a teen's views—while decreasing your positive parental influence.

key point
ESTABLISH CLEAR TIME LIMITS!

Symptoms of computer or video-game addiction:

✤ most nonschool hours are spent on the computer or playing video games
✤ falling asleep in school
✤ not keeping up with schoolwork
✤ worsening grades
✤ lying about computer or video-game use
✤ choosing the computer and video games over friends and family
✤ dropping out of social groups
✤ irritable when not playing a game or on the computer

(National Institute on Media and the Family)

Too much time with TV, computer games, or headphones can...

be detrimental to physical health.

ruin social relationships.

lead to not completing chores, homework, or other responsibilities.

Set clear rules about the amount of time each child is allowed to use media. Be sure your teen knows you want him or her to enjoy media in healthy ways. Explain that for this reason you are setting limits on how much time your teen spends with media.

key point

SET ASIDE TIME FOR FAMILY INTERACTION.

Set a limit on the total time your teen is allowed to use the TV, MP3 player, computer, or Internet in a typical day. Based on your teen's already-established media habits, you might then have to set specific rules on specific media, if he is using that one particular media outlet too much. For example, if your teen spends all his media time instant-messaging friends, limit the amount of daily time he spends online.

When asked if they have rules for media use, here's how 7th- to 12th-graders in a study responded:

> **23% have rules for how long they can use the computer.**

> **17% have rules for how long they can play video games.**

> **14% have rules for how much TV they can watch.**

(Kaiser Family Foundation, 2005)

Because your teen might initially react negatively to your limits, be consistent in enforcing those limits, along with following up on any infractions with age-appropriate consequences. If your teen refuses to cooperate, restrict or remove her media access time. And remember, it's easier to set and enforce media time limits when your teens are younger!

CHECK THIS OUT!

❖ **Be sure your teen isn't playing, watching, or listening in the middle of the night!**

❖ **Offer media time as a privilege that can be accessed after homework and family chores are completed.**

❖ **Turn off the TV during family meals.**

❖ **Spend time as a family.**

Set boundaries on where to use media.

key point
SUPERVISE YOUR TEEN'S MEDIA USE.

The decline in family time has combined with the rising number of media options to create a world where more and more teens are accessing media alone—particularly in their bedrooms. As teens spend more and more time with their media, they spend less time with their parents. Consequently, much of their interaction with media takes place in privacy, where parents have no idea what is being accessed, seen, or heard. This makes media's messages all the more powerful as teens ingest messages from TV, the Internet, or music CDs without the benefit of parental input on which media "food" is and isn't healthy.

key point
LIMIT MEDIA USE IN TEENS' BEDROOMS.

PARENT POINTER

Placing the computer and television in a common area with the screens facing outward makes it harder for your teen to access dangerous content privately. The principle is simple:

While you might not be able to regulate when and where media impacts your teenager outside the walls of your home, you can and should take steps to ensure that while at home your teen won't have free and unlimited access to media without the benefit of your supervision and input.

If there's a chance someone might look over my shoulder, I'll be more prone to do what's right.

While teenagers need the sanctuary of their own space, that space shouldn't be equipped with so many media outlets that your teen winds up interacting with media at the expense of interacting with your family. Determine which options are appropriate for the bedrooms in your house (MP3 players, stereos) and which are better suited for more "public" household access (computer, TV).

A recent study found that there is a relationship between the amount of time 8- to 18-year-olds use media and where that media is used.

	In their bedrooms	Not in their bedrooms
TV	3 hours, 31 minutes	2 hours, 4 minutes
Reading	38 minutes	54 minutes
Computer	1 hour, 30 minutes	47 minutes
Video Games	47 minutes	15 minutes

(Kaiser Family Foundation, 2005)

> **"Television has proved that people will look at anything rather than each other."**
> —Ann Landers

> How can using media in a family room help everyone share more?

To limit negative Internet exposure, set your computer in a high-traffic area, such as the family room or kitchen. Place your TV in a cabinet that closes or set it in a less-than-prominent place in your house. Don't arrange your furniture in a way that turns the room into a temple to the "electronic god." And work to replace a portion of your media time with family interaction time!

Set boundaries on content.

All media doesn't affect all kids in the same way. The level of impact varies from teen to teen depending on what's happening in other areas of their lives. Teens who are disconnected from their families or are having difficulty dealing with more serious life issues and questions are more likely to be impacted in negative ways by media's content.

key point

MEDIA CAN INFLUENCE BEHAVIOR.

Teens going through turmoil in their relationships, families, or school are more apt to be affected in negative ways by musical lyrics, violence on TV, or angst in movies.

Your responsibility is to know both your teen and his media content. Then you must be diligent in evaluating the impact that content is having on your teen. Where the result is emotional and spiritual maturity, content should be celebrated and enjoyed. But when content has a negative effect on your teen's values, attitudes, and behaviors, you must intervene to protect him or her from what's harmful and point your teen to what's good.

Remember to check ratings on movies, TV shows, CDs, and video games. Encourage your teen to do the same.

key point

BE SURE CONTENT MATCHES YOUR VALUES.

The process of setting content limits can serve as powerful teachable moments rather than occasions to spark protest. Take the time to explain your standards and walk your teen through the evaluation process that led to your decisions. Content limits should be set and an explanation offered when media's themes distort God's order and design by promoting attitudes or behaviors that are immoral and unjust.

What are the possible effects of media violence?

✦ It may lead teens to become immune to the horrors of violence in the real world.

✦ It can teach teens that violence is an acceptable way to solve problems.

✦ It can make teens more aggressive.

✦ Teens may begin to imitate violent behavior.

✦ It may lead teens to develop an unrealistic view of the world and a heightened sense of fear.

Of course, knowing where to set the limits comes from first knowing where God stands on the issues. Help your teen build a foundation from which he can discern right from wrong and truth from lies in media. Develop a growing knowledge of God's perspective by taking the time to study the Bible on a daily basis. If you skip this step, you run a greater risk of setting content boundaries that are either too wide or too narrow.

Looking for a way to access lyrical content? Check out these online lyric sites:

✦ www.lyrics.com

✦ www.azlyrics.com

✦ www.lyricsondemand.com

To monitor and view music videos online visit www.mtv. com or music.yahoo.com.

GUIDELINES & Ratings

TELEVISION SHOWS

All Children	**Good for all children, including ages 2+**
General Audience	**Most parents would find this program good for all ages**
Parental Guidance Suggested	**Contains material that may be unsuitable for younger children**
Parents Strongly Cautioned	**Contains material unsuitable for kids under 14**
Mature Audience Only	**Specifically designed for viewers over 17**

MUSIC CDs

Music CDs are not required to carry ratings labels.

Parental Advisory Label	**Contains explicit content or lyrics**
Edited Version Label	**Explicit material has been modified or omitted**

MOVIES & FILMS

G	General audience, all ages admitted
PG	Parental guidance suggested
PG-13	Parents strongly cautioned, may be inappropriate for kids under 13
R	Restricted, under 17 requires accompanying adult
NC-17	No one under 17 admitted

There aren't any ratings for Internet sites, but you do have some control over the content for your teen. Ask your service provider to find out about filters to prevent pornographic or violent sites from being viewed. Or check out one of the following for help:

> www.cyberpatrol.com

> www.cybersitter.com

VIDEO GAMES

EC	Early Childhood (for ages 3+)
E	Everyone (for ages 6+)
E10+	Everyone 10+ (minimal suggestive themes)
T	Teen 13+ (minimal blood; strong language)
M	Mature 17+ (gore; sexual content; violence)
AO	Adult Only 18+ (nudity; intense violence; sex)

Recognize advertising's strategies.

key point

TEACH DISCERNMENT IN VIEWING ADVERTISING.

In today's world, advertising is one of the most powerful media outlets shaping teen worldviews and behaviors. You must "show and tell" your teen that she is a walking target for marketers shooting at her head, heart, and wallet. Marketing to teens is a spiritual issue, as it substitutes a variety of false gospels that exploit their yearnings, anxieties, and spiritual hunger by promising to redeem and fix their lives. The reality is that marketing's promises never deliver, leaving teens unsatisfied and longing to buy more and more.

TEENS ARE A GROWING MARKET!
The teen population will expand over a million in the next few years. Imagine the spending power—and choices— our teens will face in the future!

CHECK IT OUT!

As today's teens age, their yearly discretionary income increases from nearly $1,500 at age 13 to about $4,500 by age 17. That's a lot of spending power for media advertisers to compete for!

Teaching our teens to recognize how advertising influences and manipulates their spending choices begins with making a conscious decision to pay close attention to the ads that come from every direction. Parents should practice this skill with their teens, pointing out ads and discussing the truth, lies, and propaganda whenever they are encountered.

32.4 million in 2000

33.5 million in 2010

STOP & CONSIDER

One approach that can make the process more fun is to turn it into a game. Play "locate the lie" to make those long (and often boring) TV commercials a little more exciting. It's simple: whenever a commercial comes on, see who can spot the lie first. Look for ways that the advertiser might be making the product look better than it is or be promising astounding—and often unrealistic—results.

Advertisers know that teens influence household spending. Parents consult the computer and market-savvy teens in their households for their large and small purchases.

TEEN TALK STARTERS

Is it possible that we've been swimming in the advertising "soup" for so long that we don't even know it? Joseph Goebbels, the Nazi propagandist, once said, *"This is the secret of propaganda. Those who are to be persuaded by it should be completely immersed in the ideas of the propaganda, without even noticing that they are being immersed in it."* Do you think marketing and advertising function as propaganda? Explain. What examples can you find in your own life?

As you play this game, picture the advertiser sitting on top of the TV (magazine page, billboard, CD player) in a boat and dangling over the side, a fishing line with the commercial hooked as bait. Then decide what messages and methods the advertiser is using to hook and catch you. This game will help your teen learn the necessary skills to be a discriminating media consumer who won't get hooked by silly lures and lies!

Offer media alternatives.

It's not enough to teach our teens to implement media evaluation skills or to establish media-use limits. We must go a step further by helping them fill "open" media time with positive, alternative activities and options.

Replace media time with family time.

Our busy and hurried culture has contributed to the physical and emotional fragmentation of families. Divorce and separation break up even more families. In many homes, parents are working longer hours at the expense of spending time with family members. As a rule, kids and teens do not embrace these trends or the changes they bring in their relationships with parents.

Most teens enjoy spending time with their parents. Be sure you're spending quality time with your teen away from the distractions of media.

In a typical year, kids and teens spend about 1,500 hours watching TV and only 33 hours conversing with their parents.

That's about 4 hours a day with TV and 5 minutes interacting with parents!

Instead, kids are realizing that they've been short-changed. They deeply miss and long for time spent in relationship with their dad, mom, and siblings. Whether they say it or not, all teens desire real relationships that are characterized by depth, vulnerability, openness, listening, love, and time. They long for connectedness in their confusing, disconnected, and rapidly changing world. Media often intrudes on time that could be shared together.

While it's easy for parents to "check out" after a hectic day, don't fall into the trap of plopping down in the front of the tube for the rest of the evening. Initiate family fun by playing board games or cards, working together on a hobby or craft, or shooting baskets. The key is to know your teen's interests—and to make yourself available.

With fewer families eating together, why not be a trend-breaker? Work to eliminate scheduling conflicts that keep your family from eating together. When you do sit down at the table, be sure the TV is turned off.

SHARE TIME WITH YOUR FAMILY!

Share a walk or hike.

Volunteer together.

Cook together.

Visit a coffee shop.

Take a day trip.

The key to successfully implementing shared time with older teens is to start when your kids are young. They will grow up looking forward to those fun family activities, and they'll be less prone to protest or even notice the absence of media time. When your teen is fully grown, he will realize how special and important those times really were. Your daughter may not remember the plot of a TV show or movie viewed years before, but she will gratefully remember the fun times spent with loving and attentive parents.

63%

Well over half of kids ages 8-18 report that the TV is turned on in their homes during family meals. How can you avoid media during meals?

Promote positive media options.

key point
THERE ARE PLENTY OF HEALTHY OPTIONS.

When it comes to teens and media, it's not a question of whether or not they should or will use media—we know they will! Media is a gift from God that our teens should be encouraged to use, create, interact with, learn from, and enjoy. Our parental concern is focused more on the messages media sends and how they affect our teens. Positive media messages celebrate and affirm God's truth and help us to relate to others in healthy ways. It's good, then, that there's a wide variety of nonobjectionable options available.

key point
HELP YOUR TEEN CHOOSE WISELY.

TEEN TALK STARTERS

Discuss this question with your teen: Is it possible for someone who doesn't know God to create media, music, film, or art that reflects truths about life in God's world?

Check your local Christian bookstore for great movies, CDs, books, magazines, and more!

When your teens are young, you should require parental approval for their media choices and preferences. As they mature, involve them in the decision-making process. Take time to do your research by conducting Internet searches, scanning reviews, and examining the content yourself. Internet searches can begin at www.google.com. Once you get to Google, type in the name of the film, artist, show, or whatever. You can also add the word "review" to hear what others have to say about the content. Again, encourage your teen's interest and involvement with positive messages.

If what you discover warrants a no, it's important to offer a suggestion on an attractive alternative. Don't just take one media away. Replace it with something better. You can visit the Links section at www.cpyu.org to find sites that provide reviews and suggestions for healthy media alternatives.

Don't forget that even Christian media can contain questionable content and promote values that may not match your family's beliefs. In addition, a non-Christian artist can produce media that reflects a Christian worldview even though he or she is not a Christian. Evaluate all media to determine if it's a positive, healthy media option for your teen.

HERE ARE SEVERAL EXCITING SITES FOR CHRISTIAN MULTI-MEDIA RESOURCES!

- *www.heavenandearthonline.com (Bibles, books, music, videos, and more for all ages)*

- *www.christianityfreebies.com (FREE goodies, including books, videos, gifts, music CDs, and loads more for all ages)*

- *www.ministryandmedia.com (Bibles, books, reviews, music, news, and more for 'tweens and teens)*

- *www.christianbook.com (Bibles, books, reviews, music, gifts, videos, DVDs, and more for all ages)*

Media, whether newspapers, magazines, books, movies, computers, TV, or music, does have the power to mold and change lives, minds, attitudes, and hearts. Choose and use media wisely and encourage your teen to make healthy choices based on truth, wisdom—and God's Word!

Media's Powerful Lessons

*B*ecause of where they're at developmentally, teenagers
are especially vulnerable to hearing, believing, and following media's messages. As they go through the turbulent and
confusing years of adolescence, media meets them in attractive and enticing ways, offering the guidance they crave
and answers to their many questions. As parents, we must
know what media is teaching our teens so that we can affirm
media's truths—and challenge the distortions.

Media teaches teens what to believe.

Adolescence is a time when teens investigate and evaluate a multi-
plicity of ideas and beliefs and begin to make decisions about the
spiritual convictions they will adopt as adults. Because they live in
a pluralistic world and spend so much time with media, teens are
exposed to an ever-widening spectrum of faith perspectives that
shape and influence their thinking.

Media shapes teens' concepts of God.

key point

**TEENS
LONG TO
WORSHIP
GOD.**

*B*ecause he loves us, God has revealed himself
through his Son, Jesus, and through his Word, the
Bible. Since humanity's sinful rebellion cut people
off from their relationship with God, people have
yearned to be restored with their creator. This
includes our teens. They are by nature spiritual
beings who worship either the one true God—
or a god of some other design.

With your teen, view, read, or listen to a media outlet that references God or spirituality. Filter what you've experienced by asking how God is portrayed, what you learned, and whether God was replaced with another "deity" of sorts.

Our teens are in the process of developing conclusions and opinions about who God is and what he is like. On the positive side, our culture evidences a renewed interest in spiritual things. But fewer and fewer people look to the Bible for direction. Instead, many look to media for spiritual guidance. This isn't surprising, as media disseminates information about spirituality and God (or gods) on a regular basis.

6%

say moral truth is unchanging

Do teens believe there is such a thing as unchanging moral truth?

(The Barna Group, 2002)

11%

don't know

Books about heaven, angels, near-death experiences, and finding purpose in life top best-seller lists. Many point readers to horoscopes as the source of guidance in life. Sadly, uch of the mentoring shows little or no evidence pointing teens to God or the Bible.

83%

say moral truth depends on the situation

When media becomes a type of theology class for teens, we need to be conscious of the messages this education is providing about who God is and what he's like. We must help teens distinguish what is good, true, and right from what is bad, false, and wrong.

Media shapes teens' concepts of self.

Teens spend a good amount of energy trying to find out, Who am I? When the family or church loses the desire to answer this question for teens, they forfeit that influence to media. While media has the power to give teens truthful answers to these questions, it more often than not leads them astray. When kids are told that they haven't been made with a purpose, their daily lives will be shaped by media's beliefs.

key point
MEDIA DEFINES PURPOSE FOR TEENS.

96%

of all parents of kids under the age of 13 contend that they have the primary responsibility for teaching their children values. How does media fit into what you're teaching?
(The Barna Group, 2003)

The rise in media portrayals of dangerous and risky behavior is often emulated by teens whose lack of personal value leads them to recklessly throw their bodies around. At times, media guides them to find their value and purpose by engaging freely in behaviors that are morally wrong, offensive to God, and demeaning to others. When media teaches teens to freely indulge their sexual desires without regard for God's laws or respect for others, deep and lasting lessons about human dignity and worth have been taught.

Much of the blame for the recent rise in eating disorders and steroid abuse among teens can be laid at the feet of media, which has set standards for beauty and status that are largely unattainable. Many teens are living lives where their sole purpose is to look, feel, and act like the celeb-

rity role models whose lives offer the "standards" teens believe will result in the acceptance that leads to human happiness.

Teens find references to God and spirituality on television, in film, on the radio, and in their music. Media often serves our teens as a religious mentor and life director.

Rarely are teens told by the media that they have been made by God and for God and that, if they have nothing else but a relationship with God through Christ, they will have discovered God's purpose for their lives. We must teach our teens that the Bible is clear, that each of them is made by God and not the product of chance. Realizing the wonder and joy of who "I am" involves realizing and living out who God made us to be.

"It is certain that man never achieves a clear knowledge of himself unless he has first looked upon God's face."—John Calvin

Media points teens to false redeemers.

Blaise Pascal said, "There is a God-shaped vacuum in the heart of every man which cannot be filled by any created thing, but only by God the Creator, made known through Jesus Christ." Pascal knew that when we fail to recognize that the gnawing hole in our souls can only be filled by God,

key point
MEDIA SELLS FALSE REDEEMERS.

we will try to fill it with other things. He knew that Jesus is the true redeemer through whom salvation is achieved. But media has the power to "sell" other redeemers to kids, promising them that the vacuum can be filled by more than the one true God.

Media's False Redeemers

money

"things"

love

clothing

sex

cars

fame

beer

Remind your teen that media's false promises fill our needs with empty lies!

While the message that wealth is a redeemer is present in all forms of media, it comes through especially loud and clear in advertising. Already believing the lie that "things bring happiness," our kids watch a daily parade of ads for products that promise to not only make their life better but also bring fulfillment and peace. In reality, these products can never fulfill, leading kids into the never-ending downward spiral of believing that "all I really need is more."

The percentage of Christians and non-Christians who favor the idea of making it illegal to distribute movies or magazines that contain sexually explicit or pornographic pictures (The Barna Group, 1997)

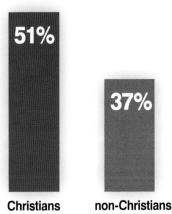

51%

37%

Christians   **non-Christians**

Because the God-shaped vacuum can only be filled with the creator, teens are especially susceptible to embracing the false redeemer of sexual intimacy. Media frequently sends the message that, when it comes to teens' sexuality, they can do anything, anywhere, anytime, with anyone—and it will make them feel better. While a few minutes of sexual intimacy might feel good during the moment, the reality is that when it's over, the vacuum hasn't been filled and will feel even bigger.

Don't forget: your teen is watching you closely! Be sure your life reflects an allegiance to and love for the true redeemer, rather than for created things.

We must take the time to help our kids understand that their yearning for God is a universal experience that can only be satisfied through embracing a relationship with God through the one true redeemer, Jesus Christ. We must explain how that universal yearning, when left unmet, will lead others to make media attractive and convincing. Teens need to know that this universal longing is easily exploited by marketers quick to make false promises of fulfillment and satisfaction.

BIG BIBLE POINT

Read aloud Romans 1:22, 23, 25 with your teen. Discuss that while we don't typically bow to the idols of Bible times, we still engage in idolatry. Make a list of modern idols promoted in media and how they are empty and false.

Media teaches teens how to live.

It has been said that art imitates life. But there is a very real sense in which life imitates art. Media's presence and power ensures that whether today's teens realize it or not, what they see, hear, and experience in and through the media influences their behaviors.

Media tells teens what behaviors are normal.

By nature, teenagers are a curious bunch. Faced with a growing array of challenges and choices, they look for direction on how to live their lives in today's world. Consequently, they are especially vulnerable to media's messages of behaviors as right, wrong, normal, and so on. Because most of these messages are embedded in stories and pictures, media's power to guide teen behavior is on the rise.

A recent survey conducted to gauge the impact reality TV has on apparel trends found that reality TV viewers exhibit an increased emphasis on sexuality, materialism, and escapism. These traits were strongest among teen viewers.

Some teens have a *monkey-see, monkey-do* relationship with media.

While media can and does at times teach behaviors that reflect God's will for the world, most research on media's influence on teens has focused on the cause-and-effect connection between media's portrayal of dangerous or immoral conduct and resulting negative teen behavior. Media is a powerful map that can lead teens on their journey through life. This often creates tension between parents who have godly expectations for their teens and teens who see those expectations as hopelessly outdated.

Media tells teens what to wear and how to look. This can lead them to adopt immodest styles of dress or unrealistic and dangerous body-image standards. When media offers depictions of sex without boundaries or consequences, teenagers are prone to initiate sexual activity earlier, more often, and in a variety of ways. Teens who view depictions of characters who smoke and drink are more prone to engage in those behaviors themselves. More and more research shows that violent media can lead kids to see violence as a legitimate conflict-solving strategy.

Nearly three out of four teens ages 15 to 17 say that sex on TV influences the sexual behavior of kids their age. (Kaiser Family Foundation, 2005)

- Limit media time.
- Monitor media's content.
- Discuss what's seen & heard.
- Teach God's truth.

Diligent and concerned parents will take steps to limit media's negative influence on their teens. We should limit our teen's media time. When they are engaged with media, we should monitor that media's content so that we are able to affirm positive behavioral depictions and challenge negative behavioral depictions. And, we should always make and take opportunities to teach the life-giving truths of God's Word as they relate to our teens' inner attitudes and resulting outward behaviors.

Media tells teens how to treat others.

key point
MEDIA
TEACHES
TEENS TO
RELATE.

As a teacher, media has great potential to lead our teens into an understanding of what it means to treat family, friends, authority figures, and those we encounter day to day in a manner that brings honor and glory to God. Because God has created all people with inherent dignity and worth, no one should be viewed or treated with disrespect, scorn, or disdain.

We should celebrate and affirm media portrayals that encourage service and love toward each other!

But all too often media encourages our teens to embrace the growing cultural wave of self-centered individualism. By denying godly values, media teaches teens that the source of their value and worth comes through personal achievement and status. When they believe that others have no inherent worth of their own, our teens can become competitive, disregarding, and disrespecting of others. They may grow to view people as mere rungs on a ladder, stepping on them as a means to an end.

BIG BIBLE POINT

Read aloud Micah 6:8 and Galatians 5:13 with your teen. Then discuss how much of media's messages ignores or refutes honoring God and serving others. Name ways media can help us serve others.

Music that objectifies females teaches our boys how *not* to treat a woman and guides our girls into a misunderstanding of how they think they're to be treated. Sexual violence and abuse will only increase when others are viewed as objects to be used for personal pleasure. When media encourages disrespect for authority, it gives kids negative lessons on how to relate to parents, teachers, the government, and even God. Media shapes how our teens relate to and treat the downtrodden, the outcast, the poor, the oppressed, the disabled, the socially inept, the sick, and people of other races.

key point

TEENS MUST LEARN TO TREAT OTHERS WITH DIGNITY.

A recent study of female African American adolescents found that, compared to adolescents who had less exposure to rap-music videos, those who had greater exposure to rap-music videos were...

1 **3 times more likely to have hit a teacher**

2 **2 times more likely to have been arrested**

3 **2 times more likely to have had multiple sexual partners**

4 **more likely to contract a new STD, use drugs, and use alcohol**

As you engage and discuss your teen's media choices with him, pay special attention to what media is teaching him about how to treat others, particularly those unlike himself. It's important to help your teen understand that, while media may tell him it's okay to use anyone for any purpose, Jesus' message turns conventional thinking upside down. He calls us to treat *all people* with dignity—to love our neighbors and to put others first.

Media tells teens what it means to follow God.

key point

MEDIA PROVIDES SPIRITUAL ROLE MODELS.

Our culture's renewed and growing interest in spirituality has created a media environment where God-talk is prevalent. A growing number of music videos, TV shows, movies, and media role models provide teens with examples of what it means to follow God. When they accurately communicate biblical truth, these depictions provide trustworthy guidance to our teens. Accurate depictions encourage teens to *"love the Lord your God with all your heart and with all your soul and with all your mind and with all your strength"* (Mark 12:30).

TRY THIS!

Ask your teen to identify a popular music icon who is outspoken about his or her faith. Search the Internet for the lyrics to that artist's latest album and read them together. Evaluate them to see if they affirm or contradict biblical truth.

While our teens most likely don't realize it, many of the examples they see cause confusion over what it means to follow Christ. In recent years, the Grammys, American Music Awards, and MTV Video Music Awards have offered a glimpse into popular music's mounting fascination with Christianity. A large number of performers who receive awards take the time to include God or Jesus in their long list of thank-yous. It isn't unusual for God to be mentioned at the top of the list.

CONSIDER THIS …

At a time when teens are forming spiritual beliefs about God, media can encourage teens to either embrace or reject Christianity.

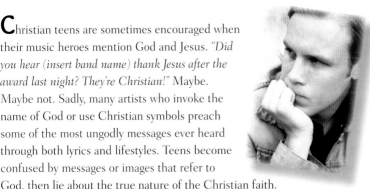

Christian teens are sometimes encouraged when their music heroes mention God and Jesus. *"Did you hear (insert band name) thank Jesus after the award last night? They're Christian!"* Maybe. Maybe not. Sadly, many artists who invoke the name of God or use Christian symbols preach some of the most ungodly messages ever heard through both lyrics and lifestyles. Teens become confused by messages or images that refer to God, then lie about the true nature of the Christian faith.

Teach your teen to evaluate Christian media heroes, their messages, and their lifestyles to see what messages they send about following God and these ten behaviors:

1. **MATERIALISM**	6. **RESPECT**
2. **RACISM**	7. **LOVE & MARRIAGE**
3. **SEXUALITY**	8. **SELFISHNESS**
4. **SERVING OTHERS**	9. **ANGER CONTROL**
5. **VIOLENCE**	10. **SUBSTANCE ABUSE**

PARENT POINTER

We must know what media messages our teens are receiving as they relate to what it means to be a follower of Christ. Discuss these with your teen, celebrating and affirming those marked by integrity and challenging those that somehow come up short.

More Resources

BOOKS

- Brian Godawa, *Hollywood Worldviews: Watching Films with Wisdom and Discernment* (InterVarsity Press, 2002).
- Walt Mueller, *Understanding Today's Youth Culture* (Tyndale House, 1999).
- Walt Mueller, *Engaging the Soul of Youth Culture: Bridging Teen Worldviews and Christian Truth* (InterVarsity Press, 2006).
- Walt Mueller, *How to Use Your Head to Guard Your Heart: A 3-D Guide to Making Responsible Music Choices* (available from the Center for Parent/Youth Understanding at www.cpyu.org).
- Walt Mueller, *Minding Your Music: A 3-D Guide to Making Responsible Music Choices* (available from the Center for Parent/Youth Understanding at www. cpyu.org).
- William D. Romanowski, *Eyes Wide Open: Looking for God in Popular Culture* (Brazos, 2001).
- Steve Turner, *Imagine: A Vision for Christians in the Arts* (InterVarsity Press, 2001).
- Sam Van Eman, *On Earth as It Is in Advertising? Moving from Commercial Hype to Gospel Hope* (Brazos, 2005).

MAGAZINES

- *Engage* (Center for Parent/Youth Understanding, www.cpyu.org).
- *Critique* (Ransom Fellowship, www.ransomfellowship.org).

WEBSITES

- www.cpyu.org (news, reviews, resources, and articles on music, media, and teen culture)
- www.ransomfellowship.org (helpful reviews and thought-provoking articles on media and media discernment)
- www.hollywoodjesus.com (information and reviews of films, with special attention paid to the spiritual content in cinema)
- www.faithnfilm.com (features daily news and analysis from the world of faith and film)
- www.lookingcloser.org (loads of film and music reviews, interviews, and weekly columns on the arts)
- www.dickstaub.com (features movie, music, book, and news reviews where "belief meets real life")
- www.mediafamily.org (site of the National Institute on Media and the Family)
- www.youthfire.com (teen chat, entertainment, movie reviews, and more)

Subpoint Index

Chapter 4: Making Media Choices 52

Chapter 5: Media's Powerful Lessons 80